MW01016078

Behold Kaua`i
Modern Days ~ Ancient Ways

Poems of Kaua`i
with
Cultural & Historical Perspectives

Dawn Fraser Kawahara

authorHOUSE™

1663 LIBERTY DRIVE, SUITE 200
BLOOMINGTON, INDIANA 47403
(800) 839-8640
WWW.AUTHORHOUSE.COM

First published by AuthorHouse 06/08/05

ISBN: 1-4208-2287-X (sc)
ISBN: 1-4208-2286-1 (dj)

Library of Congress Control Number: 2005900691

Printed in the United States of America
Bloomington, Indiana

This book is printed on acid-free paper.

TropicBird Press
Kaua`i, Hawai`i, USA

Welcome, *e komo mai,* to this book of poem-chants and insights that springs from my ongoing love affair with the Hawaiian island of Kaua`i and my resulting commitment as a writer and artist within the island community over the past twenty years.

If you are a newcomer or visitor, may this book echo and enhance your own memories of your experience of Kaua`i. If you are well-rooted in this land, may your appreciation and connection with the island be reawakened and deepened by touching into *Behold Kaua`i.* If you are far away and this book comes into your hands, may it feed an island dream and please you.

Many of us find ourselves being powerfully drawn to Kaua`i, sometimes without reasonable explanation and sometimes for a variety of known reasons. We may come on vacation to rest and replenish ourselves, swim and surf, bask in the sun and listen to the language of the sea, walk in blessing rain, fish, hike and kayak. We may move here to establish a safe, happy and passionate way of life, whether to start a new business venture or in retirement. We may come to clarify ourselves, to shed stressful layers of fast-paced living by immersing ourselves in nature and natural things. We may come to embrace our spiritual selves, or to give ourselves—our interests and knowledge and talents—to the island. Or all of the preceding, plus other reasons. What better place than an island of such dramatic beauty and friendly people?

Being "islanded" today does not mean we cut our connection with the global community. Instead of separating us, the sea that surrounds us connects us with the next land and its people, and the next and the next.

This was the guiding thought of the Polynesian navigators who became the first Hawaiians. Their sea was a shining highway to be traveled, a gift from their gods of the universe, and a purifier. Today as we set sail and fly on our own personal courses we can incorporate these ideas of the ancients, seining and selecting new paths to peace and plenty.

For two special guiding teachers and Hawaiian heart friends,
my Kumu,

Roselle Keli`ihonipua Bailey

Frances 'Hali`a' Frazier

and in memory of

Reuben Tam

who encouraged me not to let the first-draft glimpses
of many of these poems haunt me
as waste-basket ghosts,

and always,

'Dee' Kawahara

Behold Kaua`i
Modern Days ~ Ancient Ways

Poems of Kaua`i
with
Cultural & Historical Perspectives

'Miles from anywhere,
beautiful Kaua`i — come,
let her embrace you. . .'

E `Ike Mai

I luna la, i luna
  Na manu o ka lewa
I lalo la, i lalo
  Na pua o ka honua
I uka la, i uka
  Na ulu la`au
I kai la, i kai
  Na i`a o ka moana
Ha`ina mai ka puana
  A he nani ke ao nei

Behold

Above, above
  all birds in air
below, below
  all earth's flowers
inland, inland
  all forest trees
seaward, seaward
  all ocean fish
sing out and say again the refrain
  Behold this lovely world

—TRADITIONAL HAWAIIAN CHANT
Text Mary Kawena Pukui & Pa`ana Wiggin
Title assigned

The island of Kaua`i, most ancient of the seven inhabited Hawaiian islands, is the highland of a sea mount that reaches to over 5000 feet at the summit of Mount Wai`ale`ale (Rippling Water) and plummets to the depth of the sea floor. Kaua`i is joined undersea to her little-sister island, Ni`ihau, by the same volcanic action that over eons vented from this cloud-topped "mother mountain."

Though admittedly small—approximately 35 miles by 30 in width and breadth—and located at least 2400 miles from anywhere but other Hawaiian islands, Kaua`i exists as a small continent in the tropic world. There can be marked variances in rain, wind and weather patterns, noticeable "mini-climates" around the island within a framework of temperatures normally ranging between 70° to 85°.

The leeward **West Side** is sunny and hot, arid and desert-like. It is cut dramatically by the **Waimea Canyon**, which occurred during an earthquake scientists believe cleaved and reordered the land some 50,000 years ago. The highlands offer mountain haunts and greenery in the forests of Koke`e, mists and rain forest, and refreshingly cool climate. Bountiful sunshine blesses the "Mediterranean" **South Shore** of Kaua`i, which receives a moderate amount of rain and high ocean swells during summer months. The last volcanic action left a remarkable shoreline, coves and sandy bays punctuated by lava tubes, blowholes, sinkholes and craters. The **East Side** boasts the only navigable river in the Hawaiian islands, the Wailua River, rich uplands, landmark mountain shapes, sandy, long beaches and protective reefs. It basks in trade winds and preens in a balance of sunshine and rain. Kauai's **North Shore** is intensely green and lush, pelted by heavy rains and rippling with streams and waterfalls. Deep ocean swells buffet this shore during October through March. From the cliffs of Princeville past Hanalei Bay to Ke`e Lagoon, the road winds and dips over narrow bridges over which tour buses cannot pass. This factor has helped preserve the nature of the area.

Above all this natural splendor and dramatic scenery cut by wind and wave and water, the dormant Mount Wai`ale`ale reigns. The summit, measuring 400-450 inches of annual rainfall, vies for the dubious title of Wettest Spot in the World with the summit of the high peak of Cherrapunjee in Assam, India. Intermittent lowland rains refresh the land and contribute to Kauai's other name, "The Garden Island."

Kaua`i people still offer the old-style aloha and welcome to her shores. Most of the approximately 60,000 people of mixed ethnic backgrounds who make up the population of Kaua`i live in coastal towns and villages. Na Pali valleys on the northwest coast were home to the first Polynesian discoverers. Now they are part of the state parks system and reachable only by sea or by an ancient cliff-hugging trail.

This book through its collection of poems follows the way of Hawaiian chant in giving life to diverse feelings and recording events and experiences through the medium of "The Word." Like *oli* and *mele*, some poems center upon the sacred and sublime; others vibrate with human concerns such as life and death, love and loss. The collection extolls the light and dark sides of the island's personality to keep "paradise" realistic. *Behold Kaua`i, Modern Days - Ancient Ways* melds ancient knowledge and lore with modern occurrence and insight.

The poems are arranged in four geographical sections as described earlier to carry you along on this exterior and interior journey. Translations of Hawaiian words are added for easy reference, with footnotes placed at the end of poems. A selection of related cultural and historical notes are included for easy reference.

For language buffs, a list of Kaua`i place names that are touched upon within the collection with suggested possible meanings is provided at the book's end. Regarding pronunciation, a general rule gives each vowel its "long" sound, as in Romance languages. In the case of diphthongs, paired vowels, both receive a quick-slurred pronunciation unless an *okina*, the mark ` designating a glottal stop, separates them. In this case, stop the sound as when saying "oh-oh," meaning "something's wrong" (but in this case, right!).

oli - Hawaiian chants that are never danced
mele - verses set to music to which *hula* may be danced

Contents

Author's Note   v
Dedication   vii
'Miles from anywhere…'   ix
Behold (E `Ike Mai)   xi
Preface   xiii

West Side & Waimea Canyon   1

This Island   3
Mana Moonrise   5
To Koke`e   7
View of the 'Forbidden Island'   7
Kalalau   9
Lament for the Last `O`o-`A`a   12
Koke`e Cabin   14
Forest Feast   16
Waimea   18
Hanapepe Overlook   19
West Side   20
Earth Goddess   21
Kaumakani   22
December Oli   24
To the Last Stargazer   25

South Shore to Lihu'e   27

Lawa`i   29
Near Kahili Mountain   29
Tree Tunnel   30
A Return This Spring to Maha`ulepu   31
Blues Watching   33
Old Koloa Town   34
Po`ipu   34
I Know the Woman Who Ate the Turtle   35
Queen *Victoria* in the Hoary Head Range?   37

Paddling Up the Hule`ia   38
The Banyan. . .   41
Nawiliwili Harbor   42
Points of Entry   43
SoundWeaver   47
Yesterday's Lihu`e   48
Hurricane Iniki   49

East Side   **53**

A *Plein*-Air Painting ~ Beach Stroll   55
Palimpsest   57
Through the Eye of the Storm   59
Wailua RiverMouth   60
BirthStone   61
Wailua Nui Ho`ano, Great Sacred Wailua   63
Almost Home   66
Approaching Nounou Mountain (The Sleeping Giant)   68
On the Lanai   69
Tutu of the Sunshine Market   71
Dawn Chant (After Falling in Love Again)   73
Traveling North   75
WhaleWatch   76
Wearing the East Shore Down (Remembering Reuben Tam's
     painting, 'East Kaua`i Endings')   79
To Kilauea   80
Before `Anini   80
End of Conversation with a Red Crab   81
Toward Princeville   83

North Shore   **85**

SkyFest, Prelude to the New Millennium   87
Spring-Burst   89
Hanalei Overlook   91
Toward Ceremony   92
Northshore Entry   93

Hanalei Bay   93
Lumaha`i Beach   94
Pohaku   95
Road to Ha`ena   96
Love Mele   97
Ha`ena Meeting Point  (A Dream That Followed `Unike)   98
Ke`e Beach   100
Dawn at Hanakapi`ai   101
Ocean View to Alaska   103
Skeptics   104

Afterword   107
Place Names (Hawaiian)   108
Permissions & Acknowledgments   114
Major References   117

WEST SIDE
and
WAIMEA CANYON

This Island

The clouds before me
are earthborn continents, escaped —
sky-framed Australia,
grand puff of Greenland,
peninsulas and headlands,
blue Grecian isles, mapped steppes
beyond the Hindu Kush. . .

This red-green island
is all my globe now,
each detail sharpened
by close association.
Plainsland shrinks to meadow
or meadow grows to plain;
likewise, forest to thicket
river to stream, mountain to hill,

known hill
laced with personal canyons,
caves, groves, birds,
one mirror pool, one
explosion of sunrise
in the throat
of a wild, white orchid, one
aromatic sweetflesh mango.

This then, is loving the world
in an island, loving beyond boundaries
being willingly bound,
making love an exclusive art
with one consuming mistress

who leads you on and in,
caressing you with global resonances,
seeding you with the universe
with each small mystery revealed
within her

        cloudspanned
        sea-wrapped
        lava-rooted

                world,

this island.

Mana Moonrise

The hog-shaped cloud guzzles its way
toward the shell-encrusted cliffs.
Whales breach. A pod of spinner dolphins
cuts the calm between the point and Ni'ihau.

Miracles float like particles in the air.
The stars are planted—so—in the drum skin sky
that tilts above our fire.
And there,   Orion's blazing belt,
and there,   the Seven Sisters.

Sea chants fly from your throat, your guitar.

Charred steak and cheese and a round of nuts
are satisfying fare,
time flows languid as the river
as we simply stare, or sing.

The sunbrowned toddler, trusting, sleeps.

Wine and no regrets, the glowing coals,
the salty beach air, damp,
tendrils of creeping vines lead us
to our rigged blue tarp.

Toes in, we watch the sequined sky.

Constant, the curling surfbeat,
the imagined whisper feet of crabs
skimming sideways from their mounds,
and cowbells jiggling on the fishing poles.

Shocking, now, moon over the hills.

This moon proceeds along its ordained path
and verifies our spirit selves—
the world forever what it is, but a wink.
A waning moon has no regrets as it glides on,

Shadow moth of reddening sun.

To Koke`e

Rollercoaster road

rims canyons, rambles forest —

brink of Kalalau

View of the
'Forbidden Island'

The blue illusion

of Ni`ihau, cliff island,

misting dream at sea

One of the epic stories of Kaua`i that stirs the imagination and the emotions is that of Ko`olau, a brave and clever Hawaiian man. Ko`olau did not give up or give in when leprosy (Hansen's Disease), and the Provisional Government edicts aimed at those who had contracted the dreaded disease, cursed him in the last years of the 1800s.

Worthy of admiration is this young man who dared to defy orders because of his principles at the time when this was most definitely not the popular path to follow (a *Hawaiian* disobeying the ultimatum of the Americans!). Because he could not face being quarantined on Moloka`i without his loved ones, under cover of night he led his wife and child into the wilderness of Kalalau Valley in an attempt to live out life with them beside him. He knew it would not be an easy route, but he couldn't have known just what an angry storm—in fact, a small war—would break upon them following such defiance.

But let us not forget his wife, Pi`ilani, who agreed to this enforced hiding in a small and beleaguered community of lepers who built shelters in the upper reaches of the valley. She gave up all known comforts and other connections to care for her son and husband through whatever came as long as such dedication was required of her. As it is, *The True Story of KaluaiKo`olau As Told By His Wife, Pi`ilani* exists in published form, translated from the Hawaiian language by Frances N. Frazier and published in its English book form by The Kaua`i Historical Society, 2001.

Kalalau

This valley cups the blue
of salted waters to Mongolia
obscuring sunken continents, some think,
lost cities
of the ancients.

This valley holds within its basalt bowl
the taunt of green—
innocent enough
the mango, wild orange,
the burnished *kukui*
rooted through the valley saucer,
sucking moisture
hurled down random rocky falls,
secreted deep.

This valley breathes a history
of wanderers who strayed,
clung to rocky ledges
through cannon fire, refused to leave,
lived hidden
until poor, leper bones
were laid within its sunset caves.

The luring ways,
strident calls and greedy fingernails
of Earth Mother in the valley
are beauty-wrapped, though sometimes heard
or hinted at in eerie sounds
or pig-shaped clouds she steals—apparent
in the creaky sighs of cliff hung trees
and coaxing banks of misty fern
that hide trap ridges.

Wild and frighteningly wonderful
is this valley, this vessel—
Kalalau.

kukui - candlenut tree (or nut)

The lament on the following page incorporates a traditional Hawaiian chant (*Halau Ka Imi Na `Au`ao O Hawai`i Nei, Kumu Hula* R. Keli`ihonipua Bailey). Vowels are chanted to sound approx: "ah - ee - ay – 'Oh-oh' - oo."

The `O`o-A`a, a bird once prized for its small yellow puff of feathers, may now be extinct. Although repeated efforts have been made to sight or hear the call of this bird in Koke`e forests over the last twenty years, no sign of current existence has been seen or heard.

Lament for the Last `O`o-`A`a

O Hi`iaka, ke kaula nana e he ulu na ma`i
goddess in the forest, prophet in the forest
seer of things before and beyond,
O Hi`iaka, helper of Laka,
      a   i   e — `O`o — u...
Bless the birds of this place.

Other birds sip, creak and call
swoop the green streams
sail the dark waters of `Ai-Po, Alaka`i,
Tropicbirds glide the winds of the pali,
in the forest dwell shy honeycreepers,
the short-eared *pue`o* and friendly `elepaio.
Alas! no longer the flocks of lost `O`o.

Sun melts the mists, no longer will they see
light gilding the buds of *lehua makanoe*,
no longer will they feed on nectar of *koa*
and `ohi`a lehua blooms high on the ridges
or shelter hidden in `iliahi in deep mountain hollows,
no more to breathe in *mokihana* and *maile*
in the fragrant shadow valleys.

Last call fell silent in the forest,
bright, the frozen beak, the yellow thigh puffs,
still, the gloss-black feathers,
glazed, the ancient eyes.
No answer of excitement and ripening egg
the last `O`o, the lost `O`o-`A`a,
      a   i   e... Auwe!

O Hi`iaka, ke kaula nana e he ulu na ma`i
goddess in the forest, prophet in the forest
seer of things before and beyond,
O Hi`iaka, helper of Laka,
      a   i   e — `O`o — *u. . .*
Bless the birds that remain.

Awaken! bird spirits,
Kauai's feathered rainbow of song,
fly free now of danger,
claim your place in the forest,
flutter in the light, flit in your treetops,
glimmer in the sun,
      a   i   e. . .

O Hi`iaka, one more bird's gone now,
gone from the forest, gone from the planet.
Bless the birds that be. . . *Amama!*

`O`o-`A`a - a rare or extinct black nectar feeder
Hi`iaka - little sister of the volcano goddess Pele
Laka - goddess of hula and the forest
pue`o - Hawaiian short-eared owl
`*elepaio* - a species of flycatcher
lehua makanoe - a stunted variety of `ohi`a tree that grows in Kokee's
          swampland
koa - Hawaiian acacia tree
`*ohi`a lehua* - the tree *Metrosiderus collina* (and flower)
`*iliahi* – a sandalwood variety
mokihana - a native tree *(Pelea anisata)* found only on Kaua`i
maile - a native twining shrub *(Alyxia olivaeformis)*
auwe - Oh! Oh dear! Alas
amama - finished (of a pre-Christian prayer); the prayer is
          freed [lit.]

Koke`e Cabin

For Teri and Glenn

Red tin roof,
green weathered timbers,
the cabin in the clearing,
our haven.

Pictures would be extraneous on these walls—
one large window frames a grandfather *koa*
bowing and sighing through every phase of day,
while tonight the others frame stars,
the moon and Mars—very close now
like you, our friends,
sharing wine and good talk
over warmed ravioli, lime pie.
How fitting the *Clink!* of lapis blue glasses—
blue as noon Koke`e sky—
dyed purple with wine
as we toast each other
and life as it flows, *E Ola No!*

Do these walls soak up our sounds? I wonder,
examining a water stain, graph
of a thrumming winter rain, and again,
glancing at corner shadows,
Do they? as you play and sing along,
the harmonica braiding a plaintive path
through the `ukelele strum.

When we four bury our noses in books
the quiet is broken
only by each turning page. . .
                    until a gecko's chirrup
brings back my question,

What about it? I think, looking around,
If I snugged my ear up close and listened,
we-ell, what of the easy jokes
of the scouts and hikers,
good-natured boasts of trout fishermen
who have of an evening cooked and rested here?
What of our grandsons' toddler voices
babbling at play with a leaf,
a feather treasure, round stone?
And night breathing, measured as the slow stripes
of the tongue and groove?
Love murmurs, snores?

A wink before sleep carries me on
I decide, *Yes,* to myself,
dream an orchestra of cabin sounds
condensed and pent within these walls
until the beat of percolating coffee wakes me
twinned with a griddle-and-pancakes smell
within the cabin in the clearing,
mist-slickened red tin roof,
green weathered timbers
(listening, listening,
and remembering. . .)

koa - the Hawaiian acacia tree
E Ola No! - To life, indeed!

Forest Feast

Ankle deep in dew and burrs
on a mirror bright morning
we stroll the Berry Flats, snatch ripe `akala
letting the juice drizzle, lick fingertips
while craning to follow
the flutter of a yellow-green `akepa.

Round the bend, we count concentric rings
that map a sawed-off slab of *koa*,
try rolling the gargantuan wheel,
shove, but cannot budge it,
belly laugh as we careen into a ginger thicket.

A mile later we rest on a log,
wash damp grahams down with water
and stare into the dense shade of cedars.
We come upon elfen nests
some modern Menehunes have woven
of branches, ferns and mosses.
Climbing back on the road
a tardy hunting dog—
or is it the old gramophone statue?—
awaits the rumble
of his master's truck *and* voice.

We follow on to hike the canyon rim
balanced on the red edge of the world
like the lone *koa* tree
scrabbling on the burnt bare shoulder
to Waipo`o Falls.

Bagels and warm Cokes guzzled
by the pool, a cold splash
and twenty-winks on a sunbaked boulder
before we push along the switchbacks,
one bedizoned by an unexpected
seed-grown peach tree.

Up, and up still more
we labor to a crenellated ridge
drawn on by the flash, rewarded
by the chirp of the scarlet `apapane,
treble note sprung as living spark from fire,
evensong of this earth-cathedral place,
and summit view from Kumuwela.

`akala - endemic raspberries, and the thimbleberry
Menehunes - a 'little people' thought to have arrived B.C. on Kaua`i,
          lived hidden in its forests and valleys, built fitted stoneworks
          by night, slept during the day
`akepa & `apapane - endangered Hawaiian forest birds

Waimea

Kiawe chokes walls

of the Russian Fort, the bridge

skims by Cook's landing

kiawe - Algaroba tree

   In Waimea Bay the Russian American Company's ship *Bering* was wrecked in 1815. Kauai's Chief Ka`umuali`i conspired with salvager Georg Scheffer to invade and conquer Chief Kamehameha's domain with the help of the Russians. The remains of this aborted plan exist today in the site of crumbling stone walls marked as the Russian Fort on the promontory just east of the Waimea River mouth.
   Thirty-seven years earlier, in January of 1778 Captain James Cook's ships had made first landfall at the Waimea River mouth. This was on his Third Voyage of Discovery across the Pacific, when he anchored to take on provisions and water. His welcome at what was then the seat of the Kaua`i kingdom marked the beginning of official western contact with the Hawaiian nation.

Hanapepe Overlook

Gash in the red earth

bleeds the river, breathes rainbows

over the rich land

West Side

By the road now, cane.

Cane greens the valleys, more cane

ripples mountainward

Earth Goddess

This earth is alive,
　　　　we may forget
until She stretches
　　　　breathes, dances
wild and ecstatic
　　　　from island toes
to grassy plateau hips
　　　　and breasts of ancient sea beds
buttoned with corals and shells
　　　　to undergarments of basalt, granite, schist.

Her costume reflects
　　　　the warning glint
of volcano eyes,
　　　　wild, sparking hair
mood shift and boiling temper flare
　　　　of a smoldering one
pressing to erupt
　　　　from deepest anger rifts.

Daily, in every way
　　　　let us bow down and sing
aurora borealis songs to Her,
　　　　chant the wisdom
that we are but passing flecks—ova
　　　　within Her ancient flow and turn,
moon upon moon upon moon
　　　　back to our forgotten origin,
back to the beginning.

Kaumakani

Tomatoes, beans and bittermelon vines
soften the *totung* garden borders
of houses walled by cane.
Red grit blows
down the canehaul roads,
staining the sea,
the single ironwood tree,
the stones in the cemetery—

     Kane rock slabs aim skyward
     like the sugar mill stack,
     burial cairns of pitted rock,
     shards and bottles glinting in cruel sun,
     blue urn, upsidedown and cracked,
     summer lanterns fallen tattered.

Yards away, men drive by in monster cane trucks,
languid waves wash into the bay
and everything, everything glazes with salt brine,
bakes at the brink of West Kaua'i
as a lone fisherman
balanced
like a toe dancer in *tabis* on battered reef rock
throws his line.

totung - (Jap.) corrugated tin
kane - man, male
tabis - (Jap.) pull-on footwear with big toe separation, in this case fishing
    tabis with non-slip soles

December, which brings the shortest day and darkest time of the year, is the time setting of the next poem chant. The day after that shortest day marks the beginning of lengthening days, then, and the promise of the journey toward light and the longest day of the year.

The Hawaiian month that corresponds with December, according to one legend, took its name from a great navigator who steered the first canoes to the islands and was named for the constellation Makali`i (Pleiades).

These zenith stars of the Hawaiian islands were used in the science of celestial navigation. *'Maka'* means eyes, and *'li`i'* is short for *ali`i*, royal chief, so the name can be translated, 'Eyes of the Chief.'

The hero Makali`i was said to be a great farmer as well as steersman. His name was given to this time of year because it was when he set the example of planting his crops.

December Oli

Driving home from Kaumakani
and the ritual chants of hula
echoes of the drumming *pahu*
beat their way into this night,
a solstice night of inky *kapa*
dark as crushed `ohelo berries

and bunched with stars—
the "little eyes" of Makali`i—
those same star eyes that guided paddlers
from the safe shores of Kahiki
over blue-black folds of ocean
to the new lands of Hawai`i.

Now the hills and colors deepen,
towns slip by the tunnel of headlights,
gingers scent the dark with fragrance,
cane leaves rustle, shine moon silver.
Rising now, red star Ka`ula
while Kane, sun, dies past Lehua.

Your heart thrums with the season's beat
transcending miles and different peoples,
a hopeful pulse of now and ever
connecting you with those before,
those you love, the earth, each foretold star
and quickening mystery.

oli - Hawaiian chant that is never danced
pahu - ceremonial coconut log drum with sharkskin cover
kapa - *tapa;* cloth-like, beaten material made from certain tree bark
`ohelo - native shrub (cranberry family) sacred to the volcano goddess
    Pele

To the Last Stargazer

Where are the portents now,
Ulumahiehie,   where
the signs? Wrapped in *tapa* cloth
on island dawnings, island nights,
watching planets sail, and settle
            did you discern
the fallen feathers, read
Kamehameha's ending, sense
the loss of your profession. . .

            Kane of the rolling stone,
            Lono in the chiefly signs,
            Ku in clouds that stain the sky,
            Kanaloa bridging earth and ocean.

Gone, the Handsomely Adorned, gone
the *kilo hoku* of The Kingdom. Bury
those fired gourds and bones.
            It is finished, ends the prayer.

Changing patterns,
new celestial signs, alignments.

Sundancer comes now to Kaua`i,
he of Native American tribes, a healer,
holds a sweat lodge ceremony
on the earth-spine of Koke`e
while in a fancy new hotel
barefoot people chant crosslegged, incense
sweetening their workshop. The blessing
whap! of peacock feathers
wielded by the lady guru
brings with it a new awakening.

Ulumahiehie - a great priest who observed stars and forecast by them
Kane, Lono, Ku, Kanaloa - the four main Hawaiian gods
kilo hoku - astrologer, astronomer

SOUTH SHORE
to
LIHU`E

Lawa`i

Village store, flowers

at the doorway, then inside,

hot pastries, beer, bait

Near Kahili Mountain

Green pine by the road

does not yield its windward side—

short branches, and strong

Tree Tunnel

Old trees arch as limbs

reach skyward—cool green tunnel,

church, benediction

The tree tunnel that leads to Kauai's south shore has long been a landmark, a favorite postcard to mail ever since the great, corded-trunk Eucalyptus trees growing on each side of Maluhia (Peaceful) Road matured and linked their branches. These old "swamp mahogany" trees were planted to help drain the adjacent pasture with their thirsty roots.

Hurricane Iwa damaged the tunnel effect in 1982, but the leafy tunnel soon returned to its former glory. Hurricane Iniki whirled through to inflict serious damage in 1992—as with the Norfolk pine described in the previous poem. But the trees stood against the wind and lived to flourish again.

Today you can often see a car pulled off the road at one or the other end of the tunnel, with an appreciative photographer recording the landmark sight on film or disk.

A Return This Spring to Maha'ulepu

This is a shoreline walked before,
huge chunks of my life fallen, falling
as did the landmark turret of this southern shore,
rock I wanted to believe would last—
all that was left of a bridge from the past.

The cove is the same,
sands golden and fringed with pine and outbursts of Hi'iaka's
pink-bloomed glory vine,
lustrous waves of blue glass, waves of smoky blue, and ink,
blue-black pounding sledges hammering the edges
of limestone cliffs and ragged caverns
carved beside the fishermen's trail.

There, the twisted bush where a *mo'o* breathes,
wheezing death—or is it birth?—through a hidden lava tube.
There, the rock shelf where I landed a grimacing *puhi* on my pole,
looping in gruesome knots.
There, the sliver of beach
where a monk seal hauled itself to bask beside me,
sprawled alone that troubled spring.

There, the sheltered bay
where we saw whales in throbbing love display,
then scaled the chalky cliffs, plants barely hanging on—
those scrappy survivors.
And there, the fallen sinkhole that we found
and bellied down, three women stretched out side by side,
laughing on warm, reverberating stone,
our salty skins shivering
as swells slammed through and shook the very lip to which we clung
above this sweet slot of our island.

This slot's carved deeper yet—
grottoes awash, and then again awash
with forces drawn from what must be the heart
of deepest ocean
while far below, the purple urchins still hang tight.
I smile because in this endangered crack
dictated by the endless flow of currents, tides,
they thrive.

Hi`iaka - little sister of Pele, the volcano goddess; a prophet and helper of Laka,
        the goddess of hula and the forest
mo`o - lizard, dragon, serpent; water supernatural (legends)
puhi - eel

Blues Watching

The blue at the eastern edge
is the blue of the egg
I found by the trees of the bay
that other day,
then squeezed
doubting it was real.

I'm at the edge of blues
today, fragile
as that lost crack-yolk egg,
needing trust
eased back,
and vision.

Watching cyan waters
of Maha`ulepu,
you've said to see
how many shades of blue
manifest
in one full sweep. . .

Churning pools of turquoise,
light blue quiet shallows,
dark sea over ledges,
cobalt
deepening edges,
slash of a pen saying

now it's sky, now
an eggshell dome
or fabric canopy, all clouds,
all blues gathering, gathered
gone. Below
in one green swell

mates
a pair of trusting rays.

Old Koloa Town

Gray chimney of stone

marks the mill—terror and dream

of the past, distilled

Po`ipu

Palms   and sun   and sea,

beach of bright suits, fishes, kites.

'Place of crashing waves'

I Know the Woman Who Ate the Turtle

The ceremony is of the earth, *honua*. . .
The ceremony is of the turtle, *honu.*
    The women come into the clearing,
    arrange themselves in the shape of the new moon.
    They bend and kneel upon ground
    bare and brown as their dusky bodies.
    My sisters smell of jungles after rain, and glisten
    like dark stone,
        their hair, fronds,
        their lips, shells,
        cupped hands hold the sacred bowl.
    Around the navel in the center
    feet tucked beneath them,
    they bow their heads
    and breathe with the rhythm of the heart.
    A mist floats in from the sea.

Power rises from the earth
and floods their bodies,
courses up the spine, strengthens the neck,
straightens the shoulders, lifts the breast.
Power flows down
and gathers at the hips.

    The women present the sacred turtles of Ha`upu
    with a prayer,
    arranging them by age
    in the shape of the new moon.
    The ancient turtle has become an oval, lava stone.
    The younger ones wait,
    unformed, unready in their shells.

The ceremony is of the earth, *honua.*
The ceremony is of the turtle, *honu.* . .

Eyes closed, the women chant
Honua, honu   *honua, honu. . .*
The one who is to take the offering
divines
that the lava egg is hers to swallow.

I know the woman who ate the turtle!
The oval stone now glows within her eyes.
        It brings her recollection.
        It brings regeneration.
She looks toward the navel in the center,
rises to the rhythm
and dances out the beat and breath of her life.

Queen *Victoria* in the Hoary Head Range?

Spine of mountains hides

a queen in profile. *Foreign?*

Or of the island?

The humped shape of Ha`upu Mountain in the Hoary Head Range is a geologic shape that tends to draw the eye. Tour drivers of yesteryear enjoyed helping visitors locate a Queen Victoria profile on the ridge toward the Nawiliwili Harbor. The good Queen was supposedly waggling her finger, school-marm style, and saying, "No, Willy-willy!"—a laugh-getting way of helping tourists to remember the harbor name. Actually it was O`ahu's Queen Emalani who had the tie with Queen Victoria through their friendship in the mid-1800s.

Centuries before, Ha`upu Mountain was crowned by a sacred space, or *heiau.* The summit was an ideal lookout to keep watch for approaching canoes and weather. Today Ha`upu's *papale* (hat) formed by clouds more often than not translates to rain in Lihu`e.

Paddling Up the Hule`ia

Cock's crow rends the deceptive calm
of Niumalu—lapping green water,
haze-green hills, green mirrored palms. . .
The passengers from The Independence cruise
talk loudly, not noticing our quiet
in the island spell
as the group wades in, shoes in hand.
   You in new blue surfer jams,
your lop-sided grin
half admitting excitement, half cool, aloof
as you climb into the ready kayak.

We dip and turn our paddles,
slide the practice shallows,
beside us silver mullet leap—`ama`ama
of an old *hapa-haole* song.
You glide ahead of me so easily,
your dad tight-lipped between us.

The kayaks stitch a broken cord upriver,
a monster surfacing from currents
that could overturn us, drag us down.
   We work at making this a holiday,
thrusting into old Kaua`i with a leader
who sits his kayak like a chief,
like you, my son
he strokes his paddle in a sure way.

Around the bend we splash,
catching up to find him deftly slicing
pineapple to pass around
the gathering kayaks,
he points to the mangroves
strangling the fishpond,

old stonework clutched in roots
that topple well-laid walls.
      I watch you watch him
tell of rituals of death, the bone cave burials
until you feel my stare, glance over
toss back your vagabond hair,
maneuver close
to hear how his people netted fish,
so plentiful, for the *hukilau*,
steamed them in *ti* leaves, feasted.
              You shallow-dip your paddle,
intent on how the movie crews
filmed 'Raiders' in ranch grasslands,
shot the action scenes
within these banks of *hau* trees.
      Your brown eyes gleam
hearing how upstream lies the challenge
of Kipu Falls, where you can swing on vines
let go, if you're brave
plunge into swirling waters,
hoist yourself up the ladder of matted roots,
dare to dive again.

We paddle on, droplets glinting
on my sunburned skin, your father's golf-course tan.
      I remember your birth a dozen years ago
revitalized us for a spell, both of us
unable, unwilling
to say that love had died.
A touring helicopter
casts a shadow on our river path,
      I shiver in noon sun and lag behind,
wondering when the shadows
overtook the Hawaiian people,
when their energy dulled down
like mine.
      I stare right through

the abandoned dwelling,
wish the ghosts of that family back, intact,
try not to hear the jet plane taking off,
not to think of losing you
soon—so very soon—
to manhood.

Dark waters pool and spill at the dam
where we run the kayaks aground,
beside us now alights a heron,
auku`u—another omen.

`*au* — to swim, travel by sea + *ku`u* — to release, to free; *fig.* at peace

The Banyan. . .

has fingers this dawning,
fingers and hands down one section
practicing waking selections,
études of birds.

The tree hands riffle through doves now,
pulling tone from white throats,
coaxing tune through tree leaves
onto the island wind.

Playing softly when sun comes,
there are gentle splashes of silence
draping gold-green chordings,
resting the hands.

Then the fingers startle mynahs,
raucous hidden dark notes,
before glassing the run of a Chinese thrush
to its final silver bell . . .

And a truck grinds up the hill.
Gone, the hands — they are banyan branches.
Flown, the birds. Comes
another harbor morning.

Nawiliwili Harbor

Arms of the breakwall

and jetty welcome barges,

ships, tugs, small bright boats

Points of Entry

Launched into the harbor
scudding across
to the shadowshape, Black Mountain,
and the breakwall's innocent pier.
The trail sweats you
through tunnels of grasses, dry-sweet
cutting off breezes.
The trail prods you
with claws of false *kiawe*
and stands of century plants
someone halfheartedly hacked
spearing the sky.
Is this the one-in-twenty
year of bloom?

* * *

Less of a wild path now,
the views widen
across to sandy coves
and the ghost lighthouse
penciling a landing line for planes.
The walker has time to shift
the pack of water, hooks and a book,
pluck a burr,
gauge every shade of any kind of blue
before resuming
ashen marching into the sun.

* * *

Soles of the feet bake,
hot step-stone rock
down past the fishermen's sign

to the wave-washed wrap
where *opihi* thrive.
The trail goes on
if you know to read
the red mud stains, the wear
on shoulders of certain stones.
Loosened corals roll
sounding like the bones
of long-drowned sailors.
The whomp and whack of this sea
frightens, excites you.

* * *

Rising rock
prow of a ship
or an island,
whitens with summer cream,
spent waves rising
from Sitka, maybe from Nome
over the breaching whales
to the shelf
from which you have cast, have caught,
the shelf claimed by sea this day.
You climb beyond. . .

* * *

Borders run
toward this cove—
border of blue without ships,
border of lava rock,
border of cliff with its green *naupaka* brow,
border of cinder dome,
border that boils, a navel, a channel
into the womb of the world.

Only a quickening skink
or wheeling TropicBird
attest your coming
to the wild side.

* * *

90° and baked on the apron
of what was fire pit,
you cross the tube
where water forces entry,
spray hurling over rocky hips,
lips wet to several feet.
In a tide pool
cool in the gush from waves
you sit, forgetting.
You cut bait, remind yourself
to watch the sea.

* * *

The pool for a moment is still,
you are lulled, small fish nibble
and think you're an arch,
fin between the bridge of knees
while the sea, unseen,
is building, building. . .
Rogue wave
crashes over the fishbowl scene,
batters and flushes you
out of the unreal pool,
rock beneath clawing hands
becomes your enemy, your hope,
how can it be like glass,
like ice now, nowhere to hold. . . *my God!*
this is real, this is happening,

this cleft in the rock
with the surging sea,
a battering ram.

* * *

One marginal foot from the edge
the sea lets you go,
toward another point of entry.

kiawe - Algaroba tree
`*opihi* – limpet
naupaka – Hawaiian native species of shrub (mountain or seashore)
       with small, whitish 'half'-flowers *(Scaevola);* in this case,
       naupaka-kahakai, beach *naupaka*

SoundWeaver

It is a loom—
                    It is a fabric stitched with sound and light
shimmering out of a thick black void.

The storyteller folds herself crosslegged on the ground
                          after moving her loom this dawn
between the thick, rough trunks of silk oaks.
She smoothes her soft, dark blouse
                    and lifts her amulet but once,
fingering the heavy silver set of moon beads,
                          then shuts her eyes.

The webbing of sound begins to fly—
          First, the liquid green song of the shama thrush,
sweet, and punctuated with lacquer clicks,
          then, the doves interweaving their rose-grey coos
with the shocking
                knot
                    of scarlet rooster call.
                    Whispers of leaves, all gold and buff,
are leaping, now, onto the loom,
                interweaving
                    with the pewter of the early plane
and the raw brown sound of trucks.

The soundweaver sits with her sleek head bowed,
                    her shuttle hands still and her eyes turned in.
She smiles an enigmatic smile
             as over and over the soundweave loops and overlaps
and fills the loom of day,
                        glinting here and there
with threads of music, laughter, loving voices.

At dusk the woman lifts the weave,
                      casts it sailing into velvet skies.
Then she re-strings her loom before she wakes for night.

Yesterday's Lihu`e

Town and sugar mill,

Lihu`e ambles, or sleeps—

sweet molasses smell

Hurricane Iniki

September 10, 1992
    Day Before

Heavy, the morning.
    A carport cleaning binge!
    I sweat, stamp nervous roaches,
    wipe down the shelves, chase geckos.
    Breath comes hard.
    By 2, my hair, electric.
    3:30, showered and dressed
    I'm driving to work past my mountain,
    Ha`upu,
    notice a purple-grey poi-dog cloud,
    wild jaws to the island,
    dim howl in the offing
Heavy, the air, thick as Jello.
    No breeze through the gallery windows,
    I sell no artworks, there are few questions.
    The visitors flit from vase to painting,
    scarcely hover by prints
    before moving on to dine—
    What is this we're feeling?
Heavy and long, the evening.
    9 o'clock, I fasten the windows,
    lug in frames from the hallway hooks, take a last look
    at all the neatly placed and feather-dusted contents,
    set the alarm, and lock.
    Outside, stillness.
    Cars in neat rows await their owners
    lingering over demitasse and brandy
    on the restaurant veranda.
Heavy, the night, overcast,
    the dog cloud has guzzled the sky,
    no sign of Orion.

Keys held ready, hurry into darkness
past leaden leaves on witchy bushes
marking the employee's lot—
no one is lurking. Rolling home
I know my sweetheart's waiting,
he'll have lit the light for me—
Why is the hair on my neck still rising?

September 11
Morning

Sirens wake us, pierce my dream.
You do not shave,
we do not brush our teeth.
No time for coffee, hurry down the hill.
The lines for gas are long.
Batteries, none. No candles,
hardly any tape, we grab 2 rolls.
Pile a case of saimin on our cart,
Quick! Cans of beans, soup, corn.
Don't forget powdered milk,
toss oranges into a bag.

At home, Dave's fed the cat,
stashed his surfboard and the garden bench.
X is the spot, I think, as you tape Xs on windows,
teeter on chairs,
hammer nails *rat-tat-tat!* into quilts.
Fill jugs, jars, buckets, the tub with water,
all the Tupperware, even the washing machine.
1 hour to go. Cushion and pad the hall,
our bunker. Stock it with snacks, bandaids,
the camp lantern—(the radio crackles)—
batteries.

Brian calls. 'You're having a hurricane?'
        'It's on the *Cleveland* news?—Yes. . .'
(I'm in a hurry for the hurricane.)

        'Not yet. It's very still right now.'

        'We're staying put. Don't worry. . . (static)
hello. . . Can you hear me?'

When he was young and the kids went wild
I used to wish for peace, for quiet—
but not this kind,
this incommunicado rush toward the warning hush
preceding hurricane.

September 12
Day After

First cry of a bird,
light filters into my wind-&-whirlpool dream,
open our eyes, the room sunlit, the chaos now calmed,
lone dove calling us out of our damaged house,
coaxing us to witness
what was an orchid tree in latent loveliness,
now a fractured skeleton,
blooms ripped from bare brown twigs,
shredded by the winds
that raged, swirled and tossed
any above-ground thing,
mixed every shade of leafy green
to paste upon remaining walls,
a ghastly hand turned to the task of creating
salt-water soaked collages

51

we can hardly bear to see
fashioned of wood and wire, glass,
face cream jars, cassettes,
tiles, whole beams, skewed poles,
trophies, photos, dishes,
tangled skirts and shirts,
broomsticks and hangers, bandannas, *all my books*
not to speak of the neighbor's top storey
set down *Plonk!* before us in the road
and the A-frame on the other side, collapsed
(without the neighbors in them, *thank God!*),
close by, a car stripped open
like a scrap-heap sardine tin.
Along the trail, no wild chickens scurry and squawk,
an albizia branch lies slammed across the bridge,
I watch my husband stroke the blaze
on the velvet nose of the grazing horse,
'It's all right, fellah,' he says—All *right?*
We can walk no further in the maze of fallen trees,
we can drive no road to town,
the sheltering green hills stand stripped, dull brown,
ravaged not by war or fire storm
but the vagaries of nature when forces clash.
We never may live so carelessly again
on beautiful Kaua`i.

EAST SIDE

A *Plein*-Air Painting ~ Beach Stroll

Sand between the toes again,
your footprints first, then mine
winding a sandpiper song
along the curving sea bowl line.
You find a minute shell—
a pearl-stained fingernail,
I veer around you in wave-washed space
defined by distant coves and cliffs
blue-gray in twilight
and clouded, mauve.

Passing raindrops pock the strand,
send swimmers lunging into riffs
or hurrying to huddle in limp towels
in the shelter of sea grape trees,
picnickers coax damp fires
under the spilling lid of sky.

We revel in the cool,
the washing/sloshing sounds
as surf wraps our ankles,
the sink and pull at our soles,
we scramble over rolling bones
of Northwest cedars—
bleached flotsam to our shore,
we dart around fishing poles,
toss broken shells back to the reef.

Near the condos a woman
shyly beckons, holds up her camera,
you click her posed in the black sarong.
*What a lonely silhouette,
a 'wish-you-were-here'—don't you think?*
I murmur, looking back.

I run my palm down your forearm,
squeeze your warm hand,
you walking in step beside me.

Around the bend
a sandcrabbing dog
bounds from the pit he's dug
on legs so short we join in laughter
with the couple perched on a log,
their plate lunch chopsticks
poised, mid-air.
A sun-red youth
stares right through us
as he splashes toward the big hotel
followed by a pair of frowning
talk-talk-talking men.

Back to the car
we brush sand off our feet,
a man pulls up in a rental van,
his neon shirt flaps, unbuttoned,
in the wind
as slowly he turns, videos
the scene silvered by last light
on this beach
that is our evening whim.

Palimpsest
(Commemorating 9-11-01)

We look upon our island,
see dark shadowing of Tuesday—
black September Tuesday
in New York, Washington,
a burnt field in Pennsylvania.

The twin peaks
that mark our Anahola mountain,
mnemonic,
the ragged trough the wild pig roots
amid upland *ili`au*, ravaging one
s l o w   jungle chicken.

We come upon another shock
along Wailua greens—scattered feathers
attached to wasted flesh,
remains of an unwary plover
arrived in a daze to what seemed paradise,
savaged in the 'land of plenty.'

Scraps of paper
crazy-dance the ditches, roads,
tide-knitted piles of twisted driftwood bones
grate, they keen
of stricken beams and rubble, the shocking collapse
of individual and collective dreams. . .

Outdoors on our garden island
we find it futile
to seek relief in nature
from images burned and buried in us
from a far coast we cannot sever.

A layered palimpsest
of terror unforeseen
surpassing by far *our* 9-1-1 nightmare
nine lives, nine years ago—Hurricane Iniki,
lets us not forget.

*ili`au* -a plant found only on Kaua`i, related to the silversword

Through the Eye of the Storm

Our houses, downed around us, our things, but salvage,
after the storm I grasped the wisdom
of transmitting knowledge through the word,
the well-remembered chant
instead of books, now mildewed paper pulp.
Whatever I know is stored within me until the death of mind.
This, an ancient land, hilltops thrusting into the sky
have held those shapes and looked for a thousand years
and more, much as they look now.
I see stone walls, foundations that the First Ones built,
spaces that stand defined as clearly as in those ancient times
while the tumbled *hale*, tower and *ki`i*, rotted thatch
are all ephemeral as flesh and bone encased by skin.
In darkening wind and tidal wave
the rock   the place   the people and their word
the lashed gourd, and all acts of heart   outlast the storm.

hale - house
ki`i - image

Wailua RiverMouth

Deep ocean surge swirls

lehua and *hau* blossoms

around guardian rocks

    The ancient name of Wailua Bay was *"Ka-Lehua-a-Wehe"* (The Fully-Opened Lehua Blossom), intimating someone who is fully ready (for love-making). A traditional *mele* (song) tells of the royal colors of the yellow *hau* (hibiscus tree) blossoms floating intermingled with the red of a beautiful *`Ohi`a Lehua* tree of surprising size that blossomed underwater only.

BirthStone

By the sacred river
came the women to the birthstone
in their ninth moon. . .

    Coaxing, chanting,
    the *kahuna* hovers
    drawn into the wails, grunts,
    screams of the *wahine*
    by the river, the great Wailua.

    Bearing down, fluid spilling,
    pumping tides
    propel each folded lump of breath and tissue,
    bones apart, stretching, pulsing,
    rush of blood, flesh, bone,
    comes the babe, comes the cord
    still knotted to the *mana* of the First Ones,
    chiefs and chiefesses of Pele
    in their long canoes.

    Strike the bellstones,
    ring the message of each new child
    to all people
    through the sacred valley
    to the Mother Mountain's summit.

        Woman in her journey to the birthstone
        is all water, every boat and oarsman.
        Woman resting from the torrent
        feels the hollow sound within her, floats
        the quiet pools of river, channels
        the echoes of the bellstones.

kahuna - priest, or expert in any profession
wahine - woman
mana - supernatural or divine power
Pele - the volcano goddess

This next poem came to me as a *mele* (song) in praise of the rich river valley and uplands of Kaua`i in which my husband and I make our home. Po`Ele`ele, which is often mistakenly called "The Bellstones," is the place with a view to sunrise where we were wed on a summer solstice dawn. Kumu Hula Roselle Keli`ihonipua Bailey guided us in planning a ceremony appropriate to the occasion and the site.

In one of those strange ironies life deals out, it was less than a mile upland from that place of a joyous beginning, seven years later, where I thought my life was to end. For that reason, "Almost Home," the poem focused on that dark and painful experience, follows in sequence.

"Wailua Nui Ho`ano" names the seven *heiau* (sacred spaces) that were built over a long span of time. Even in the face of a modern overlay there still exist segments of ancient walls and marker stones along the Wailua River from its Eastern Shore to its origin at the summit of Wai`ale`ale. The *heiau* name verses honoring these places are intended to sound like the percussive beat of an ancient Hawaiian chant.

Wailua Nui Ho`ano
(Great Sacred Wailua)

Wailua—
where two waters join as one,
golden valley
kissed by rain and gentle sun,
Wai`ale`ale
of the silver ribbon falls
births the river
to the east.

Wailua—
with your streams and waterfalls,
fragrant forests
where the shy bird often calls

from the fern beds
and the gullies carve black shadows
down the sides
of sunlit cliffs.

Wailua
Nui Ho`ano—
sacred valley
where Kaua`i chiefs of old
followed the river
to the summit and the source,
hailed the gods,
wondered at stars.

> Hikina A-Ka-La,
> Mala`e, Ka-Lae-Manu,
> Po`Ele`ele, Poli`ahu,
> Pihana Kalani,
> Wai`ale`ale. . .

Wailua Nui Ho`ano—
walled by mountains,
lined with fertile valley soil,
he wai e ola!
home to tropicbird and owl,
heaven on earth—
we praise you!

Kapu Mountain
hides a grotto hung with mist,
caves and ridges
form the *mo`o's* natural bridge,
and the moon floats
hidden by radiant rainbow capes
teasing the hill
of Mauna Hina.

Wailua—
where the full moon lights the trail
over Nounou
at his feet, `Opaeka`a Falls
and the cold pools
where the warrior spirits roam
along the banks
on the nights of Ku.

Hikina A-Ka-La,
Mala`e, Ka-Lae-Manu,
Po`Ele`ele, Poli`ahu,
Pihana Kalani,
Wai`ale`ale. . .

Wailua—
where two waters join as one,
golden valley
kissed by rain and gentle sun,
Wai`ale`ale
of the silver ribbon falls
births the river
to the east.

Wailua—
sacred channel flowing east
brings fresh water
to mix and mingle with the sea
Wailua
Nui Ho`ano
blessing your people,
we praise you!

He wai e ola! - The water of life!
mo`o - lizard, dragon, serpent; water supernatural (legends)
Ku - one of four major gods, represents war; from Tahiti's *Tu`u*

65

Almost Home

Somehow I miss three beats of Mozart up the hill,
after the waterfall, before the turn,
                    and you, a block away
as the car meets the pole beside the wall—
stopper - *jolt!* - sound shocker
streaks - flashes as steel grinds wood
becomes a crumpled metal page
imprinted by a nightmare embosser,
glass shatters, my heart convulses
unplugged, hotfire moving drain,
ribs mashed to the wheel, crush of pain—
My sister! Open one eye, engine in the empty seat—
Safe! Dropped off. Thank God.
                    You, my home, a block away. . .
slipping, slipping away,
I have done it to myself—my whisper
lamenting the raveled threads,
love unmade, words unsaid,
stories untold, unwritten.

A man's voice, *'Easy now.'*
'Anyone else?'—my breath held,
picturing neighborhood kids
who hang out here under the avocado tree.
'No,' his hand upon my forehead,
'you're gonna be okay.'
I shudder, *'My husband. P'lease,'*
pointing past the pole
'Noni Street. . .' the house number gasped.
Right away he sends a boy for help, dials his cell.

The sound of running, slowing down,
a woman's voice, close by me now—
'Darned window's jammed.'
Her arm squeezed through,

she fans me with her cap, slow metronome.
> Good people.
> *Good people!*
'*Nothing to see, go on along,*' she tells someone
draped over the wall, gawking.
I close my eyes,
breathe. . . coast. . . float. . .

Your voice, near and nearer
saying my love name
before the sirens swoop,
your magnet touch flies away my pain
as the homestead rooster
flaps in the blue-light haze.

Approaching Nounou Mountain
(The Sleeping Giant)

Awake! and place your feet upon the trail,
your forward movement more important than the goal.

You leave the folded pasture with its morning
cows, dip down to stride across the bridge
that spans the chortling stream, its roughcut
timbers slick with mountain mist and rain,
below, you read the signs of last night's flood,
the flattened grass, wrenched logs and tumbled timbers
frame randomly the once clear, lazy pools
where skulk dim shapes of trolling bass.

Across the bridge the mountain looms, treed outline
lit by sun as though airbrushed with liquid
platinum, four hulking trees
stand sentinel while pea and sheep-eye vines
festoon the river thicket and a riot of mountain
apple blossoms drapes a tree skirt of magenta
to feather the fecund earth. You stop, arrested
by this beauty, breathe deeply of this scent, this paradise.

You start to climb now, bowing your head
to walk the winding tangle of tunneling trees,
you enter a sudden darkness, a damp dim side
of your paradise, a hidden dell that spawns the mushroom,
mosses, mold. But, also, fragrant fern beds,
bursts of native *hala*—pandanus trees—and among these
legions of brown-gold toads and shy, sweet songbirds
burrow and nest, feast the layers of sponge and leaf.

In a flash, you grasp the basalt mountain's cloak
of softness—earth form of your bone and masking flesh.

On the Lanai

For Joy & Jim

It is a night
with Venus swinging from a crescent moon
and Orion studding the sky,
beguiling our eyes.
Earlier, over wine
the silken quilt of this night
softened, settled down—
sunset pinks glazed a burnished sea,
       then deepened,
              darkened to indigo,
the heavens, echoing.

We sit back after feasting
four friends
humming in our sense of unity
with self,
      with each other,
           and with our world.

Lizards arrive
to tend the lights
wreathed in the vernal warmth of May
by termite swarms
gobbling
      bugs
         greedily
as we gulp random beauty.

Each attendant thought
   and sound
      and star

is, as the wise man said,
'right with the world.'

lanai - porch, veranda

Tutu of the Sunshine Market

Between bouquets of lettuce,
beans and bittermelon,
eggplant and yellow globes she calls *jabon*
she crouches on her heels,
folded, much as she was born,
now creased as a leaf,
skin parched in Kaua`i sun
an ocean away from her girlhood home.

Today she's planted herself
under the rainbow umbrella
between the taro man's truck
and the lei lady's stand.
      '*Two dollah,*' she chants,
      '*Two dollah—sure you no like sumting moa?*'

Tutu tucks away bills
in a fold of her wrap,
slicks wisps of wiry hair
from middle part to knotted bun.
In the slack between sales
she steals a drag on a green cheroot
shared with her old sugarcane man.
They weed, they hoe
their camp house plot
in a daily pact with life
sealed with their toil.

For the farm market strollers
who stop not to eye or pinch
and bargain down, but to buy,
her crinkled hands
cradle fern shoots, bundle
sprays of dragon-eye fruit

and banana flowers into Big Save bags
while he counts out garlic bulbs
and pungent ginger nubs.

Reflections in *Tutu's* garden eyes
mirror what she knows well
of seeds, of harvest seasons, of drought
and bargains struck
with the earth.

jabon – pomelo (pumelo); shaddock, grapefruit variety
Tutu - Grandmother

Dawn Chant
(After Falling in Love Again)

For Dee

First rooster —
      first rooster calling, then
the first light of morning,
      first rosy light, then
the first clouds,
      first clouds piling like purple *kapa,*
      first bird,   <u>then</u>
      first sun over Ke`alia. . .
            Day is born!

Light breathes life into the dark valley
warming the stream
vining the trees with green —
      plum and mango, monkeypod, *hau* —
The breadfruit draws deeply,
      lifts arms to the sky.
Rain comes, a blessing.
The red road muddies
      and the ripe earth steams.

This day
      first blossom unfolds
      banana leaf unrolls
      prawns in the ginger roots
      fish in the pool
      and you can get drunk
            on the fragrance of guava. . .

This day, this life
      sun has come to Ke`alia
      light has come to Ke`apana,
      bird drinks the flower

and the yellow-black spider
             goes on spinning the web
                  of the world. . .

kapa - tapa; clothlike, beaten material made from certain tree bark
hau - a lowland tree *(Hibiscus tiliaceous)*

Traveling North

Anahola dreams

in the hollow of mountains—

heaved humps of dark stone

When nearing the Hawaiian Homelands area of Anahola the upland mountains dominate the scenery. The peaks of this range are described popularly and in legends. The most prominent peak, Kalale`a, was often called "Hole in the Mountain," but since erosion has filled in the hole, the shape of the peak has been likened by some modern travelers and tour drivers to the hulking head and shoulders of "King Kong."

A writer friend who was drawn to relocate to the island because of the energy and effect of this particularly peak upon her, imaginatively describes the Anahola mountain shapes as a woman lying on her back, her hair flowing toward the water, with Kalale`a, the shark at her throat. At times I am able to visualize this from as far away as the Lihu`e Airport area.

However, if I view the high peak's distinctive shape as anything but what it is—a stand-out geologic feature of Kaua`i that was praised and revered by Hawaiian people—I prefer to see it as one of the spires of ancient holy sites at which I have marveled. These were constructed in Cambodia, Thailand and India to symbolize the fabled Mount Meru by armies of laborers and artisans over hundred-year spans, not by the volcanic action and erosion since first emergence that formed Kalale`a.

WhaleWatch

I — October

Along the Anahola coast the mud road bends,
we watch for the whale that's beached itself,
through cane we catch a glimpse of sand, of rock
and hear the surf above the wind.
   Hauna! the sudden stink invades us,
   makes us second-guess our quest,
   there on the reef rock past the makeshift shack
   lies a soapy hulk now marbled with red iron veins—
   no more a gleaming whale
   roaming as spirit chief of its sea home,
   its foundered body bubbles greasy suds
   instead of splash and whale song.
Saddened, we stay just long enough
to photograph, holding our breath
while trying not to see the ragged flukes
where sharks have bitten this great beast
chasing it, hastening death
on the clamorous current.

hauna - odor of rotting fish or meat

II — January

The rains have souped the four-wheel-drive tracks
of the seekers drawn to view the whale remains
much as people throng to a wake, a funeral viewing.
   In the fall we questioned
   how 'whale' could mean the thing we saw,
   lifeless mound.   What of it now?

The stench, when the wind shifts inland,
the shack, collapsed,
the dirge of waves in the cove
scouring a fence of vertebrae
foaming in the rock pool.
        Crabs dance eulogies at moonrise, shells
        and stones roll through the rancid pelvic bone,
        we are held, gripped by this finality
        of whale-spell.

III — September

Whales, mother and babe, beached
then buried shoreward of the golf course dunes.
Walking the strand, we imagine the mighty back-hoes
covering lives reduced to cartilage,
wasted, and endangered, *yes!*
        A waking dream of high school kids,
        chattering mynahs on excursion,
        decked out in shorts and rubber slippers
        with bleach and scraping tools and brushes
        come with their teacher
        to gather for their learning lab,
        set to scrubbing in a corps
        like so many Dermestid beetles
        cleaning scraps off ancient bones
        in sealed museum cases,
        sweating, the youths strain to roll
        their separate finds onto the waiting tarps
        and sing their rappy songs.
The desire to daydream the whales back to life,
their consciousness refitted,
re-linked, the puzzle of disjointed bones.

IV — Reprise

Rumor has it that a trophy hunter claimed
the jawbone of 'our' whale, chain-sawing it,
but mother sea completes the reclamation,
once more our Anahola whale
glides back into the ocean.

Cup an ear, look to Alaska—
Is that an echo of the whales' last song
keening on the wind, spindrifting?

Wearing the East Shore Down
(Remembering Reuben Tam's painting,
'East Kaua`i Endings')

For Gerry

Waving yards of watered silk
ruche and rumple,
fumble, snag on rocks,
frill the bays and inlets,
ruffle the rustic stilts of the pineapple pier,
wearing the East shore down.

Walls of blue glass crawl,
hammer and shatter,
explode diamond water
while hungry currents tear off,
grind and swallow chunks of lava rock,
eating the East shore down.

Waves mirror whales
mating and birthing beyond the bays,
rising and falling in frenzied love display
as tubes break, turn, churn,
bashing the East shore cliffs,
melting the shoreline down.

Dragged by the bold, blue moon
the current builds,
the high sea swells of ink and deep merlot
swirl to pounding froth.
This very moment under a tie-dyed sky
the East shore's wearing down.

To Kilauea

Fields, flower-banked homes,

the lighthouse proud on its point.

Sea, always. And birds.

Before `Anini

Hala trees thicken,

lush river valley, but first

splash the waterfalls

hala – the pandanus or screw pine *(Pandanus odoratissimus)*

End of Conversation with a Red Crab

So, Crab with your spinning eyes,
they're building six more homes
at Aliomanu, sixty or more at Donkey Beach.
No impact on the reef, they say,
since conditions here are different
from that *other* island's bay.

Six more homes, maybe sixty-six
instead of six more shopping centers, after all,
people need a place to stay.
It is a question of degrees, then, Crab,
you understand,
                    a dune, versus a grain of sand.

Who's to say what's causing the surface scum,
the death of coral heads, gray underwater dreadlocks
trailing from every rock, the screaming absence of fish?
Your home was 'sea life heaven'
less than thirty years ago
alive with piscean shapes in colors
that surpassed the jeweled visions of inspired dreams.
Who's to say the change was due
to run-offs from garden and golf course sprays?
Perhaps a subtle dose of human waste?
                    What? —*Nah*, they say.
Crab, before I walk on, let me say
I see our meeting together as one—
me, the curious bi-ped, you, the lone crustacean—
our life net anchored in deep ocean
yet stretched taut to skyhooks past the moon.
Within us both
flow tides that are the same—salt pulse,
salt wind, blood water of the universe.

A sudden wave assaults my sandy feet,
Crab skitters and plunges to wedge his shell
into a crevice of the reef, waggles
a fishhook claw, stalk-bright eyes.
A relentless current flushes him
in a raft of scum bubbles.

Toward Princeville

Horses and riders

gallop the seaward pastures,

white egret rises

Princeville, a present-day cliffside development built in and around golf courses and located between `Anini Beach and Hanalei Bay, was named in honor of Crown Prince Albert of Hawai`i, who was destined to become Kamehameha IV.

Albert Edward Kauikeaouli Leiopapa A Kamehameha was welcomed with a twenty-one gun salute at his birth in 1858. He was the godson of Queen Victoria, who had developed a friendship with his mother, O`ahu's Queen Emalani. Sadly, Prince Albert died in childhood, followed by the untimely death of his father, Kamehameha III, leaving the Queen bereft as a wife and mother.

In happier days, Queen Emalani and her husband had traveled to and enjoyed the scenic area now called Princeville as part of an official visit. The Hawaiian royal family had also brought the infant Albert back to share their joy with the people of Kaua`i on a subsequent official visit.

After losing both her son and husband, the Queen returned to Kaua`i and spent a mourning period at a family home in the Lawa`i Valley. When she returned to official duties in Honolulu, she continued the work she had begun with her husband to insure better medical care for her people. Queen's Hospital in Honolulu is named for her.

NORTH SHORE

SkyFest
Prelude to the New Millennium

All day the coming of the March full moon
teases and beguiles,
at twilight, pulls us gliding to the point.
You cut the engine, slide into the one remaining space
surprised by the gathering crowd—
dared we dream that we'd be the only ones
to come here singing lunar music
along with rising silver tides?
Laughable—yes?—to think that we, alone,
are feeling magnetized
to one more cliffside view
of these star-badged, star-buckled skies.

Friends bunch in pastel tufts,
lone Buddha statues meditate cross-legged,
families with roly-poly babies and dogs
entrench themselves on mats
with coolers and cameras.
Weedy flowers sprout among the rocks,
lovers nestle in niches.
Three small boys flap by in rubber slippers,
hop the wall through the clump of students
milling around high-powered telescopes.
The roadway jams,
someone asks what's going on.
The moon, we say, pointing to the horizon,
an eclipse of the moon.

Tripods are steadied, lenses polished,
the sea foams far below,
light leaks away,
the sea-grape leaves blur, become
black lacquer plates.

You reach for my hand,
I wish out loud that the clouds would break,
that we could see the moon rise,
shake a fist at the purple yam clouds
but they just sift and scud
while arrows of light pierce dark sea.
Still, we stare with those around us
seeking to glimpse the shadow of our earth
although it seems a heavy door's clanged shut
between the moon and plunging sun.
Look! you urge me, *Look behind us!*

The sparkler comet steals the show,
we turn toward this ember
blazing in the northern sky
seeming to scorch the hilltops,
now drawing every eye.

Spring-Burst

In the island months
ruled by cloud and current
and lengthening night,
the tree we pass on our walks
like us, hunches over in the drizzle,
slickened by pelting rain,
its trunk stubbled by lichen—
an old man's chin grizzle.
    When the sun slows,
    riding higher, bolder
    in the mountain saddle
    and the vines and fronds
    shake like rattails in the gusting winds
    the oldest leaves let go,
    curling brown and mottled.
    We kick at them, walk briskly by
    hanging on to our caps.
        As the waters warm
        and the whales swim home
        we rise to walk in early coolness,
        drink in the delicate dew.
        The antler patterned branches
        of our old man tree reveal soft nubs
        of new leaves big as your toenail
        or your cupped heel.
            Behold! one porcelain morning
            every once-bare tip of our neighbor's tree
            opens to light and warmth, renewed,
            bursting with petal crowns
            and floral stars—
                we break stride (how could we *not?*),
                stop, wonder
                at the fragile passion
                of pink, gold-and-cream-hearted

incomparably fragrant
spring
plumeria blossoms.

Hanalei Overlook

Kalo in paddies

where rice was grown. Wade herons,

coots, and red-legged stilts

kalo - Hawaiian for taro staple starch plant *(Colocasiaesculenta)*

Toward Ceremony

The hill, breast of our mother, the earth,
and the moon egg born above it, Hina
beating her glowing tapa.
Naupaka flowers matched and mindless of Pele's wrath
we go to our knees, bow to each separate self
before we travel,
> roughest stones, vagaries of heart behind us
> smoother flows ahead, and shine—
>> glints of olivine and flint, and drifts
>> of Pele's hair—

a glimpse of what the path now brings,
pale shells cupping the soles of our flying feet,
on our heads, ceremonial feathers,
at one heart, two fluttering birds.

Pele - a 'foreign' goddess to Hawai`i; Pele represents earth power evidenced in
    Pacific plate volcanic eruption and lava flow, destruction and creation
Pele's hair - spun glass threads, volcanic byproduct
naupaka – Hawaiian native species of shrub (mountain or seashore) with small,
    whitish 'half'-flowers *(Scaevola)*

Northshore Entry

One-lane bridges to

fabled places—Hanalei,

Lumaha`i, Ke`e

Hanalei Bay

The old pier crumbles,

daily the bay spawns its fleet—

forty pleasure boats

Written before the pier's reconstruction and new regulations limiting tour boat operation.

Lumaha`i Beach

Not surf, lava rock,

nor summer lagoon, nor strand

were fashioned by man

Pohaku

Water wraps rock
sheening Pohaku,
woman of stone flanks,
swirling in eddies
trickling through tidepools.
Here in the splash zone
gobies go darting
past sea cucumbers
lazing and rolling
near the pale seaweed
near the pink urchins.
Hermits are feeding
scuttling old shells,
seaworms' white strings
feel out each crevice
here in the splash zone
trickling through tidepools
swirling in eddies
blessing Pohaku,
she who chose to be
woman of land
and woman of water,
water
       wraps
            rock. . .

Pohaku, according to legend, chose to be part of both land and
sea as reef rock, unlike her two brothers, who left the sea entirely to
become land rock.

Road to Ha`ena

Through the *kamani*

always the dark cliff, looming,

dim caves of Pele

Pele - the volcano goddess
kamani (-haole) - Indian almond trees *(Terminalia catappa)*

Love Mele

Tideline sand, it seems
is made for walking
just as toes, and soles, are made
              for sand. . .

     Take my hand, fingers twining
     I will lead you
     under my secret *hala* tree
     near the lagoon, spread
     our *kapa* cloth scented
     with fern, wait
     for the sun to die, the birds'
            'coo-roo'—
     sweet as a nose-flute melody—
     feed you well, Love, weave
     you the island moon.

mele - verses set to music to which *hula* may be danced
hala - the pandanus or screw pine *(Pandanus odoratissimus)*
kapa - *tapa;* cloth-like, beaten material made from tree bark

Ha`ena Meeting Point
(A Dream That Followed `Unike)

Trusting the stars, two sailors have come,
strong, weathered men in tanned skin and tattoos
hurry now, leaving their vessel at anchor
follow the path of lava rock cobbles
through leaves and lianas fringing the sand dunes
to the place of the keeper of Ke-Ahu-a-Laka.

The cliff scene seems strange, yet somehow familiar
as they approach a hidden dwelling.
       'U-i. . .'—the voice of a woman,
they startle, think, then, 'This is the day. . .'
       'E komo mai!'
This, then, the voice, an echo of welcome
heard many a dream-tossed night.

She wears a wrap of softest *kapa*
yellow and red as the heat of Ha'ena,
and strands of ferns, green life of the forest.
Her great, dark eyes with sun-whorl pupils
are the eyes of Woman—
priestess, sister, lover.

The men are curious, draw close as she beckons,
watch her peel layered leaves
off a basket—brimming with lizards, stiff, dry lizards!—
in the shade of the clearing.
Their eyes lock as she answers questions
flooding their heads, not yet spoken,
      'The *mo`o* have lasted long in island salt
      stained by the healing red `alaea.
      You will offer these. . .'
      (she points to the cliffside) 'for Laka,
      She of the forest,

Goddess of *Hula*,
    daughter of earth, the great Goddess Mother.'

Her breath a fragrance on their faces,
they shuffle their feet like untried youths.
One of the sailors hefts the basket, they follow
her bare feet skimming the rocks
of a twisting, hidden trail. She hears their footfalls,
hopes that she has trusted well.

On the final ascent to the grassy platform
rimmed by the moss-rock wall
she pauses, smiles in secret
because the sign for which she's waited
appears, stock-still, before her toes—
a living lizard
marked with linking diamond shapes.

One breath, one saurian blink of its eye,
then it slips between the stones
into a crevice of ochered bones.

'unike – graduation ceremony and recital for hula (or other ancient arts)
E komo mai! – Welcome!
kapa - tapa; cloth-like, beaten material made from tree bark
'alaea - red dye from high iron content of red earth
mo'o - lizard, dragon, serpent; water supernatural (legends)

Ke`e Beach

Road's end, ancient trail

begins. Here the sacred place

of Laka, *Hula*

Laka - goddess of the forest and *hula*
Hula - the ancient religious worship, through chant and sacred
    dance, of light, and enlightenment

Dawn at Hanakapi`ai

One ripe guava
thuds down the lean-to
bursts pink star seeds,
enough for a pungent grove
of trees.

Sky bursts into morning
pouring silver and indigo
into the sulky sea
that droned us
past campfire time
when sparks burst, popping
echoes of exploding stars.

Bellies and canteen, full,
muscles sore from the pack
but our spirits
fish this valley view
like the red-tailed TropicBird
careening by shipstack cliffs.

Summer sea caves beckon,
the sand lies yet untracked,
the morning view, pearlescent,
gilding the cool rock dome.
We squeeze through a dripping arch,
rub wet stone lichen colors.

Small fish zip the lagoon,
moss grows near the secret spring,
toads lie coupled,
their jellied egg ropes
quivering, soon to burst

like last night's Hina moon.

Hina - goddess of the moon

Hanakapi`ai was once known as the "valley of the weavers" of natural fibers—in particular, the *lauhala*, or specially prepared leaf of the *hala* (pandanus) tree, which grows prolifically in the North Shore area. Today the name "Hanakapi`ai" refers to one of the first rest or camping stops along Na Pali (The Cliffs) trail after beginning the hike at the Ke`e Beach trail head.

Care must be taken in crossing the stream that separates the rocky beach from the trail, especially after downpours on the mountain, when the stream current strengthens. Beach safety signs should be obeyed: this is not a swimming beach. Even the best swimmers thinking to cool off in shallow waves have suddenly and unexpectedly been dragged out to sea by deep ocean currents. With rescue teams and help having to come from far, the history of drownings and disappearances is a sad one.

A rigorous hike upstream into the valley leads to a waterfall. Wild coffee bushes that have grown into trees date from an early attempt to grow coffee commercially on Kaua`i.

Ocean View to Alaska

The whales have returned—

breaching, singing, churning the sea

of their tropic home

Skeptics

Sandals sliding along
      the sloping mat of grass
            toward the curve of sand,
warm, your hand in mine,
salt breeze rumples our hair, chills our skin
as the sun falls out of a winter solstice day—
last of the century.
We do not hurry toward sunset.
The spangled sea splashes foam,
      dashes, lays bare
            walls of buried sandstone.
High waves launch a steady assault
against the black and jagged cliff
that marks the end of the beach.
Cloud veils sift, the sun bounces once,
      rays stabbing the line of cool blue at the western edge,
settles, slims to a narrow disk,
      thin
            and thinner still—a fiery slice
      slipping,
            slipped below horizon,
transformed, becomes an emerald prism.
We blink and stare
held by the spell of that slow jeweled wink,
stand vesper still,
then lift our arms, whoop, giddily spin,
splashing along the silver fringe
of the cove's dusk roll and tumble of velvet purple.

When colors merge to gray on gray
your fingers lace through mine,
leading me home slowly.
As if at a signal
we both glance back toward the darkened portal

of that iridescent green flash
      we've longed to see
            but half-believed as myth
and only, now, perceive as lucid magic
presaging our new millennium gift.

Some people shrug and laugh at the mention of the "green flash" of a clear evening, scoff that tales of such a happening are only make-believe. Those who have seen the phenomenon would like to discount a scientific explanation—that is, that the yellow-gold of the setting sun seen only for seconds through a translucent window of blue hues at the horizon produce a fleeting green vibration.

Rather, we offer you the inherited view from Polynesians who became the Hawaiians, the first peoples of this land. In this type of view, every facet of life is sacred. Prayers of thanks are offered in gratefulness for all that is clearly seen and fully experienced by people of the islands—

> moon, stars and planets, sun
> wind and tide, seasonal changes
> ancient goddesses and gods
> `aumakua (guiding spirits)
> people, creatures
> rocks—molten and formed
> `aina (land, earth)
> plants, trees, fruits and flowers
> sands, seas, waves
> water in all forms, including rainbows (night and day)
> gifts of dreams and inner voices
> inspiration and creativity

All of the above, and more, are seen as being joined, just as islands are linked to each other and larger continents by global seas. All are integral parts of the magical, interconnected voyage of life as we live and perceive it. Everywhere in the world, throughout the universe, in a continuum. Before us, and long after.

Behold Kaua`i!

Place Names

Please note that because of the ancient age of many of the place names in this book as well as the fact that the Hawaiian language was a spoken language—not a written and punctuated language with added diacritical marks—many of the meanings given here are suggested only. Although the `okina (`), or glottal stop is used in this book to aid with pronunciation as accepted today, following the renascence and reemergence of the language from its American English overlay, the *kahako,* or dash placed over vowels—which can greatly affect meaning—is not.

It is hoped that readers interested in information about the place names of Kaua`i as mentioned in this collection of poems will gain a sense of the rightness, the appropriateness after considered thought that was at the base of the clever and complex Hawaiian art of naming. For readers who wish to delve further there exist various books and reference works that in comprehensive and scholarly fashion focus on place names, origins, and meanings.

**`Ai-Po** – A dark swamp of highland Kaua`i.

**Alaka`i** – A swampland area in Koke`e.

Aliomanu – An east shore area; *manu* refers to shark(s).

Anahola – An east shore area and community; to measure the hour; hourglass.

`Anini – A beach shore area east of the Princeville cliffs; to vary, as great and small waves.

**Ha`ena** – A north shore area of Kaua`i; red-hot, burning, red.

Hanakapi`ai – "Valley of the Weavers" on Na Pali coast.

Hanalei – A large north shore valley, town, and crescent-shaped bay; lei valley.

Hanapepe – A valley and town on the west side; to bruise or crush.

**Ha`upu** – A dominant humped peak in the Hoary Head Range south of the Lihu`e area; to recollect, recall, remember.

**Hawai`i** – In Polynesia this name, sometimes paired with second term, refers to the underworld or ancestral home. In the islands of Hawai`i today the name holds no meaning.

Hikina A Ka La – A *heiau* (sacred space) area that was built at the Wailua Rivermouth; to the East rises the sun.

Hule`ia – A stream flowing into Nawiliwili Harbor; a kind of soft pumice stone.

Kahiki – Tahiti; the horizon; any foreign country (over the horizon).

Kahili – A mount in the range inland of the Tree Tunnel leading to Koloa; a feather standard (sign of royalty); a rainbow standing like a shaft (also a sign of royalty).

Ka-Lae-Manu – A *heiau* (sacred space) built into a rise beside the Wailua River (also known as Holo-holo-Ku); the cliff of the birds.

Kalalau – A valley on Na Pali coast; to go astray.

Kalale`a – A distinctively shaped mount in the range above Anahola on Kauai's northeast side; the joyous sun.

Kapa`a – An east side town presently with the most population; the solid; the dry and rocky.

Kapu Mountain — Taboo Mountain marked the boundary of the sacred and royal district of Wailua.

Kaumakani – A sugar plantation camp town of west Kaua`i; *kau*, to mount or ride on, *makani*, the wind.
(Ka Imi Na Au`ao O Hawai`i Nei *halau hula* [The Search for the Truth of Hawai`i hula institute] was located in Kaumakani while Kumu Hula R. Keli`ihonipua Bailey resided on Kaua`i. Today it is based on Maui, with national and international branches.)

Kaua`i – This name is so ancient, its meaning has been forgotten. Some think it may point to a place of plenty, or a place to come to rest (as the setting sun).

Ke-Ahu-a-Laka – A sacred site dedicated to the goddess Laka above Ke`e beach and lagoon on the northwest coast.

**Ke`alia** – "The Salt Beds" beach area north of Kapa`a town.

**Ke`apana** – A valley area inland of Ke`alia; a land parcel, part of a larger *kuleana* (land division).

Ke`e – The northwest coast beach and lagoon at road's end; a crooked turn, fault, flow.

Kilauea – Kauai's northernmost community and peninsula; a place of (long ago) great volcanic eruption (as in the presently erupting Kilauea of the Big Island).

Kipu – Rolling green ranch lands southwest of the Lihu`e area; to rein in, as a horse; to remain, as mist or rain; tranquility.

**Koke`e** – The mountain area, today comprising Koke`e State Park; to wind or bend (such as the approach roads).

Koloa – A south shore town famous for churches and whaling; long cane with a crook.

Kumuwela – A ridge beyond a cliff and valley trail of Koke`e; source of heat.

Lawa`i – An inland town on Kauai's south side; to have enough, be satisfied.

Lehua – A volcanic crescent islet off the sand spit on the north end of Ni`ihau island.

Lihu`e – Today's county seat and main market town, adjacent to the airport and Nawiliwili Harbor; "place of chill breezes."

Lumaha`i – A long sand beach with a steep and dangerous drop-off on Kauai's north shore; a certain twist of the fingers in forming string figures.

**Maha`ulepu** – A dramatic, as yet undeveloped southeastern coastal area of Kaua`i which may have been connected with winter solstice rites in ancient times; "all falling together," which may refer to the human bones buried in the sand dunes.

Mala`e – An ancient rectangular *heiau* (sacred space) in the Wailua District; clear and calm; a clear field; serene, as a cloudless sky.

Mana – An arid, desert-like place on Kauai's western shore.

Mauna Hina – The Wailua District's Mount of Hina, the moon goddess.

Na Pali – The Cliffs.

Nawiliwili – Kauai's major harbor today; named for the

wiliwili trees *(Erythrina sandwicensis, formerly E. monosperma)* that used to grow in abundance in the area, the light wood of which was used for surfboards, canoe outriggers, and net floats.

**Ni`ihau** – Ni`ihau Island; *ni`i,* salt-encrusted, *hau,* native hibiscus tree.

Niumalu – A valley area inland of Nawiliwili Harbor; shaded by coconut palms *(Cocos nucifera).*

Nounou — The 'Sleeping Giant' Mountain feature of Kauai's east side.

`Opaeka`a Falls – The Rolling Shrimp Falls of the Wailua District.

Pihana Kalani – Gathering Place of (high) Supernatural Beings.

Po`Ele`ele – An ancient pair of megaliths in the Wailua District facing east; the (dark) realm of the gods; formerly, the period of 24 hours beginning with nightfall (the Hawaiian "day" began at nightfall).

Po`ipu – A south shore community and popular beach park; to cover entirely (clouds or engulfing waves); to attack, overwhelm; an onslaught or attack.

Poli`ahu – A large *heiau* (sacred space) thought to have been constructed by the Menehune people on a promontory over the Wailua River; bosom goddess; to caress (rare).

Wai`ale`ale – Rippling (fresh)water. Almost constant rain fills the pool atop Kauai's volcanic mountain and causes ribbon falls to cascade.

Wailua – Two(fresh) waters becoming one; a place of spirits.

Wailua Nui Hoʻano – An eastern area of Kauaʻi bordering the Wailua River; "Great Sacred Wailua."

Waimea – Reddish Water; the name of a west side bay and town.

Waipoʻo – A Waimea Canyon mountain waterfall; freshwater depression.

Permissions & Acknowledgments

Thank you to members of the Kaua`i Writers Group—'The Sands of Tam' for patience in hearing and critiquing many drafts of numerous poems, and particular thanks to Frances Frazier, Joy Jobson, and Teral Katahara for first reading of *Behold Kaua`i* in manuscript form.

Mahalo nui loa to all community friends who continue to encourage and support poets and poetry. A special *mahalo* to Beryl Blaich, Frances Frazier and David Helela for sharing insight on puzzling and obscure place names, and to Francis X. Warther for his special insight in the field of archeo-astronomy as it relates to Hawaii's sacred sites.

Thank you to the University of Hawai`i Press for the use of "Behold *(E Ike Mai)*," *The Echo of Our Song: Chants & Poems of the Hawaiians* tr. and ed. by Mary Kawena Pukui and Alfons L. Korn, UH Press, 1973, Honolulu, Hawai`i

"Pohaku," *Fire in the Sea*, ed. Sue Cowing [UH Press, 1996]; and the Kaua`i writers and artists anthology, *Now We Are Islanded Together* [Magic Fishes Press, 1987]

"Almost Home" was published in slightly different form in *Jackals' Wedding, A Memoir of a Childhood in British India,* Dawn Fraser Kawahara, [1stBooks Library, 2003]

"Approaching Nounou Mountain" won Hawai`i Pacific University's James M. Vaughan Award for Poetry, 2002; published in HPU's Hawai`i Pacific Review, Sept. 2003

"A Return This Spring to Maha`ulepu" was awarded first prize in the first Malama Maha`ulepu Poetry Contest and was presented at the Garden Island Arts Council Poetry Fest-2003; it was awarded third prize in the National Federation of Poetry Societies Annual Competition—1997 (Mass. State Poetry Society award)

"SoundWeaver" won the Hawai`i National Writers Group—Honolulu Poetry Contest—1992 and was published in the Writers Group's publication, Vol. 1, No. 9

"I Know the Woman Who Ate the Turtle" won third prize in the California State Poetry Society Aug. 1989 Poetry Contest; it was presented with hula & percussion instruments at the first Na Lima Kakau (The Writing Hand) at Kaua`i Museum, Sept. 1989; published in Garden Island Arts Council "ARTS," Jan. 1990

"Blues Watching" and "The Banyan" were published in the Kaua`i writers and artists anthology, *Now We Are Islanded Together* [Magic Fishes Press, 1987]; "Blues Watching" was presented at the International Peace Day Celebration—1988, State Building, Lihu`e

"Miles from anywhere. . ," "To Koke`e," "View of the `Forbidden Island,'" "Waimea," "Hanapepe Overlook," "West Side," "Lawa`i," "Near Kahili Mountain," "Tree Tunnel," "Old Koloa Town," "Po`ipu," "Nawiliwili Harbor," "Yesterday's Lihu`e," "Traveling North," "To Kilauea," "Before `Anini," "Toward Princeville," "Hanalei Overlook," "Northshore Entry," "Hanalei Bay," "Lumaha`i Beach," "Road to Ha`ena," "Ke`e Beach," and "Ocean View to Alaska" published (some in slightly different form) in *Memories of Kaua`i, A Tour of Kaua`i in Music and Poetry*" cassette recording by the poet with music by Stephen Nichols [Southern Seas Band Publishing Co., 1987]

"SkyFest, Prelude to the New Millennium" won a poetry award in New Millennium Writings—1997; it was presented at the Kaua`i Mokihana Festival—1997 "Mele Mokihana"

"End of Conversation with a Red Crab" was published in a slightly different form in the "Poets Corner" [The Garden Island, Lihu`e, 1985]

Performance & Readings

"A *Plein*-Air Painting - Beach Stroll" was read and displayed as an art visual at the Garden Island Arts Council Poetry Fest—2004 "Shape Poem" Exhibit

"Earth Goddess," "Love Mele," and "Spring-Burst" were presented for the

Garden Island Poetry Fest—2003. "Love Mele" was originally presented in "Woman Chants Her Heart" [1986 YWCA-Kaua`i annual program]

"Skeptics" was read and displayed at the Garden Island Arts Council/Chiron Arts Poetry Festival—2002, "Poetry for the New Millennium"

"Palimpsest" was written to present in honor of the first Hawaiian Arts and Culture class of travelers post 9-11, Hawai`i Pacific University Elderhostel [Wailua, Sept. 2001]

"Lament for the Last `O`o- `A-`a" was written and performed for the Kaua`i Mokihana Festival—1998 "Mele Mokihana"

"Through the Eye of the Storm" and "Hurricane Iniki" were presented in slightly different form at the one-year Iniki Community Blessing Ceremony [Sept. 1993, YWCA-Kaua`i]

"Dawn Chant (After Falling in Love Again)" was performed for the Kaua`i Mokihana Festival—1990 second Na Lima Kakau (The Writing Hand), Waipa, and the Garden Island Arts Council's Poetry Fest—2003

"This Island" was read in performance at artist A. J. Metzgar's "See What You See" show opening reception, with the poet presenting original poems with poets Reuben Tam and Beryl Blaich [1987, Kilohana Galleries]

Major References

Hawaiian Dictionary, Pukui, Mary Kawena and Elbert, Samuel H., Revised Edition, UH Press, Honolulu, Hawai`i

*Unwritten Literature of Hawai`i, The Sacred Songs of the Hula*, Emerson, Nathaniel B., 1998, Mutual Publishing, Honolulu, Hawai`i

Hula instruction—chants, dance, protocol—and Project Kilo Lokahi related research and field studies (1985-1994), Ka Imi Na Au`ao O Hawai`i Nei, Kahiko Halapa`i Hula Alapa`i (To Excite in the Ancient Ways of Hula), Kumu Hula Roselle Keli`ihonipua Bailey (www.kaimi.org)

Original research and course syllabi written by the author for Hawai`i Pacific University's Elderhostel Hawaiian history and culture classes (Pacific Islands Institute), 1997– present, ongoing.

Other works by Dawn Fraser Kawahara

Books

*The Kaua`i Guide to Artists & Their Art,* 1988, Magic Fishes Press, Lihu`e, Hawai`i

Jackals' Wedding, A Memoir of a Childhood in British India, 2003, 1stBooks Library, USA, C. Dawn Fraser Kawahara. (www.authorhouse.com) A winner in the Writers Digest International Self-Published Books Competition, 2004, Life Stories Category

Audio Cassettes

Memories of Kaua`i, A Tour of Kaua`i in Music and Poetry, original poems (haiku) and recording by the poet, with music by Stephen Nichols, 1987, Southern Seas Band Publishing Co., Lihu`e, Hawai`i

Pele's Riddle: "Where are the Waters of Kane?" narrative script, with members of Kahiko Halapa`i Hula Alapa`i (To Excite in the Ancient Ways of Hula) narrating, chanting, and playing instruments, Ka Imi Na Au`ao O Hawai`i Nei, Project Kilo Lokahi, 1994

Museum Exhibits

Co-authored with Francis X. Warther: *Pele's Riddle: "Where are the Waters of Kane?"* exhibit story on ancient Hawai`i: "Building the Sky: Cultural Astronomy with Oli (Chants) of Ancient Hawai`i 1993," staged under the auspices of Ka Imi Na Au`ao O Hawai`i Nei, Project Kilo Lokahi, with Hui O Laka, exhibited at Koke`e Museum of Natural History (1994) and Kaua`i Community College (1995), Kaua`i, Hawai`I

Liz Fricker

Dawn Fraser Kawahara

During her writing career Dawn Fraser Kawahara has freelanced enough articles to line myriad birdcages and taught herself how to write prize-winning short and long fiction. She has authored *Jackals' Wedding, A Memoir of a Childhood in British India*, www.authorhouse.com (2003, 1stBooks Library), a winner in the Writer's Digest International Self-Published Books Competition 2004, Life Stories category. She won the James Vaughan Poetry

Prize 2002, Hawai`i Pacific University, and has received numerous awards from the National Federation of State Poetry Societies.

Dawn published the Kaua`i Guides and an anthology of poems by island poets with art. As Poet-in-the-Schools, Kaua`i, she encouraged students to fall in love with language and experiment with verbal and written expression. She is the originator and curator of the annual Garden Island Arts Council Poetry Fest. She dedicated herself to the study of ancient *hula*, its chants and sacred dance, and presents readings and workshops based on the unwritten literature of Hawai`i nationally and internationally.

When her inner gypsy gets restless, Dawn leads travel groups in Pacific journeys under the auspices of Hawai`i Pacific University's Elderhostel program. She is also an instructor, teaching several Elderhostel course lines. When not at home "with birds and books," she and husband Delano love nothing better than traveling the world to photograph and learn of the sacred sites of ancient peoples.

LaVergne, TN USA
15 June 2010
186265LV00002B/11/A